P9-DMI-147

# SIMPLE
# MATTERS

## JUST ABOUT EVERYTHING
## YOU NEED TO KNOW
## ABOUT LIFE, RELATIONSHIPS,
## AND KNOWING GOD

# BRUCE & STAN

PROMISE
PRESS
An Imprint of Barbour Publishing

Published by Promise Press, an imprint of Barbour Publishing, Inc., P.O. Box 719, Uhrichsville, Ohio 44683 http://www.promisepress.com

 Member of the
Evangelical Christian
Publishers Association

Printed in the United States of America.

# CONTENTS

# INTRODUCTION

Within your lifetime, the world has gotten progressively more complicated. Technology has played a big part in this, but it is not solely to blame. Our society as a whole has stepped up the pace of living. As the tempo of our existence accelerates, the logistics of life itself become more complex. We have more places to go, more things to do, and more people to meet. While the urgency of these matters increases, the time in which to do them seems to diminish. It is difficult to fit all of your living into your life.

Although this frenetic pace can be somewhat stimulating, there is a danger that the important things of life may get neglected or forgotten. The things that matter most in life are never complicated, and they are seldom urgent. They don't evolve through stages of increasing intricacy. They are simple, and they stay that way. That's what makes them easy to overlook. Perhaps we tend to ignore their truth and value because we mistake their simplicity for triviality.

This book is all about those simple, yet important, aspects of life. The insights in the following chapters are more basic than innovative; they are more fundamental than theoretical; they are more traditional than experimental. That's the whole point. The important matters of life, relationships, and knowing God are simple. They aren't new or improved because they are timeless. In fact, you probably already know many of these principles, but it is our guess that you haven't thought about them for awhile (because you were too busy remembering cell phone numbers and computer passwords).

If your schedule seems out of control, if your world is spinning too fast, or if you are increasingly dissatisfied with your circumstances, then disengage from it all for a moment. Adjust your perspective by reconsidering the simple matters of life.

# LIFE

*Maintain your focus
on the simple,
yet significant,
things in life.*

# Common Sense

*It is extremely embarrassing to come to your senses
and find out you haven't any.*

*If* you are like most people, you spend a significant amount
of time watching television. You probably feel a little guilty
about it because you know that most of the programs are a
total waste of time. In an effort to appease your conscience,
you rationalize all of the time that you spend on the couch
in a semivegetative trance by pretending that you are actually learning something. So, for you, television watching
isn't a waste of time; it is an educational adventure.

Sure, you can expand your storehouse of knowledge by
watching the Discovery Channel and PBS. We'll even give
you academic credit for watching the Travel Channel. (A
little geography is mixed in with the list of the Top Ten
Beach Resorts.) But if you think that you are learning
about alternative dispute resolution techniques by watching
*The Jerry Springer Show,* you are kidding yourself. And do

you really think that *The Antiques Road Show* is going to sharpen your consumer skills for those Saturday morning garage sales?

Let's admit it: Much of what you need to learn in life will not come from watching television. And it won't come only from reading books, either. The important things you need to learn happen in real life. As you live your life, you learn from what happens to you. As you accumulate life experience, and hopefully learn from your mistakes and successes, you begin to attain an elusive and rare quality: common sense.

Education is wonderful, but common sense is better. An education (whether obtained in the classroom or from the television set) can provide you with facts. But many of those facts don't have much relevance to everyday life. When it comes to real life, you will need to rely on common sense and good judgment much more than on what you learned from watching that PBS special on male pattern baldness.

You may think that common sense is such a simple matter that it doesn't take any effort. It is true that common sense comes naturally for some people. But whether you are well endowed with this quality or seeking to obtain some, there's a tricky aspect to common sense: It is easy to overlook. Often, in the excitement of the moment, it gets forgotten. We know that you would never let that happen to yourself, but you might know a few people who need to bring a little common sense to their activities. For them, common sense can be a simple matter of asking a few pertinent questions, such as:

**❶ *Is it safe?***
This is a good question to ask whether you are thinking about jogging alone at night or changing a flat tire on the side of the road. Here is a clue: The danger in some activities is blatantly obvious (such as juggling chain saws), while other activities are more subtle and deserve a little forethought.

**❷ *Who came up with this idea?***
Talk to anyone who has been swindled out of some money. They got talked into doing something by someone else. You know better than to get involved with someone who is on parole from an embezzlement conviction, but even prospective dealings with your neighbors and friends

deserve a few additional moments in contemplative reflection.

❸ *What's the worst thing that could happen?*
Think through all the possible scenarios. If any of them involve obituaries, CPR, police lineups, or losing your money, then make sure you have weighed the pros and cons.

❹ *Will this seem like a dumb thing five years from now?*
What seems like a great idea now may be considered complete idiocy five years from now.

❺ *Will God be pleased?*
This doesn't mean that you can't have fun. Just the opposite. We are convinced that Jesus used to laugh it up with Peter and John and the rest of the guys as they were walking from town to town. But whether we are being serious or just goofing around, we should remember that God is involved with what we do.

# LIFE

Common sense can be like a shy friend. It kind of stays in the background. Sometimes it can get lost or overlooked in all the excitement. But it is a friendship that should be developed and nurtured.

Make common sense your best friend. Take it with you wherever you go. It will be invaluable to you—because it may save you from making some costly mistakes.

# Focus

*Just over the hill is a beautiful valley,*
*but you must climb the hill to see it.*

The activities of your life can be dangerous to your vision. We aren't talking about an ophthalmologic problem that can be remedied with corrective eyewear. We are referring to the hectic pace of your daily schedule that blurs your focus on what is important in your life.

We are confident that you could quickly list the things that are important to you. For instance, family and friends probably rank very high on your list. But if you were to analyze the activities of your daily routine, you might be depressed by the tiny fraction of time that you get to spend with the people who mean the most to you. The pace of life seems to drive people apart when they would prefer to be together. Each person is operating on his or her own schedule, and it seems that you have to make an appointment to share a cup of coffee. (And getting your schedules to coincide for an entire meal is often downright impossible.) Having time for a leisure conversation with your spouse or your children or your friends is a rare privilege, and it is often cancelled due to unexpected conflicts in your schedule or theirs. Whether it is working late at the job, making a quick trip to the dry cleaners, or making time to pay those pesky bills that have been accumulating during the last four weeks, you probably find that you are so busy doing those things you *don't* enjoy that there is no time left to do the things that *would* bring you joy.

Don't despair. Don't let the routine of life discourage you. Much of what you do each day may seem boring and mundane, but don't let that obscure your vision of what is important. Sometimes we can't change *what* we're doing— but we can become more aware of *why* we're doing it. Stay focused on the significant things in your life.

If you analyze your activities, you are likely to find that they do revolve around what is important to you. Your job, those trips to the dry cleaners, and even those bills you are paying at midnight aren't really disruptions and distractions. Instead, they are necessary components of your activities that connect you to your family and friends.

You are likely to enjoy your life much more if you view your activities in the context of what is important to you. Maintain your focus on the significant things in life. Don't get distracted by the busyness. Instead of dreading all those things you have to do, consider that those activities are part of what you are doing for the people you love. By focusing on what is important to you, the other things will no longer be an annoying distraction.

It is all a simple matter of focus.

# Laughter

*With the fearful strain that is on me night and day,*
*if I did not laugh I should die.*
ABRAHAM LINCOLN

*This* book is all about the simple matters of life. But don't make the mistake of thinking that you don't have to take these matters seriously just because they are simple. Sometimes the simplest matters in life are the most serious. Laughter is exactly that—a very serious matter.

Laughter is an essential part of life. You already know that it is fun to laugh. You enjoy it; it is pleasurable; it puts a grin on your face and encourages your spirit. But forget about yourself for a second. (Everything isn't always about *you*.) Think about how important laughter can be to someone else. Most people could use a little cheering up. They could use a little laughter to brighten their otherwise dreary day. You might be the best person—perhaps the only person—who can bring a little laughter into someone else's life. Don't miss that opportunity.

Because laughter is such an effective means of improving your life as well as that of those around you, you should work diligently to hone your sense of humor. A sense of humor gets rusty unless it is used, so don't keep yours buried beneath a bunch of neurotic personality traits. Let your sense of humor shine through. But you must learn to use it wisely. Used properly, a good sense of humor and the laughter it brings can work to your benefit. It will. . .

- make your own life much more enjoyable;
- make your family and friends enjoy your company more (because you'll be fun to be with); and
- disarm people who are angry with you (because every body likes a person with a good sense of humor).

A sense of humor can be destructive, however, if not used properly. So you need to be careful how you use it. Here are three simple rules for laughter and humor:

**❶** *Laugh at yourself.*
You will always be your greatest source of humor.
Don't ever take yourself so seriously that you can't
find humor in the things you say and do. Of course
it's easy to laugh at yourself when you do something
embarrassing. For men, this usually entails walking
around with your zipper down. For women, it may
happen when you unknowingly tuck your skirt into
your pantyhose before you exit from the restroom.
(We don't know this from personal experience, but
our wives tell us that it is every woman's greatest fear.)

**❷** *Laugh with others.*
Some people can't (or won't) see the humor in their
situations. Other people may not be as comfortable
with their goof-ups as you are with yours. Make sure
they are laughing before you get started. If they start,
then join in; if they don't, then suppress your laughter (but be careful not to blow out your eardrums).

**❸** *Laugh often.*
Laughter is good for your health. It releases tension
and stress. It has physical and mental benefits. How

do you think George Burns got to be so old?

You will find that laughter removes all barriers. When people are laughing together, there are no age differences, no racial barriers, and no economic distinctions. It is just people enjoying their existence.

A sense of humor is a valuable asset. Appreciate it in yourself and in others. We're serious about this.

It's no laughing matter.

# Health

*The human body, with proper care, will last a lifetime.*

*Your* health, good or bad, will affect everything you do. It impacts your relationships with your family, your performance at work, your recreation, and your social life. If you are feeling great, then all of those things will be better. If you're feeling lousy, then everything you do will seem that way, too.

Health is a simple matter, but it is also commercialized and exploited. You can't change channels on television without seeing an infomercial about some new dietary supplement, a drain-the-fat-away cooking gadget, or some exercise contraption that looks like a medieval torture device. But these items hawked on TV make staying healthy seem much too complicated. We need to keep it simple—so we have to admit that our nutritional supplements consist of a latte from Starbucks; our fancy cooking apparatus is nothing more than a barbecue (on which the fat easily drains off between the bars on the grill); and our weight-lifting and flexibility exercises consist of lifting a briefcase and crawling into a subcompact automobile.

Nutrition and exercise are important elements of a healthy lifestyle, of course, but we suspect that most people are ignoring the most obvious element of health: sleep. Getting enough sleep is probably the most important part of staying healthy, yet it's such a simple matter that it's easy to overlook.

When you are tired, you are irritable. When you don't get enough sleep, you lack sufficient energy to make it through the day. In short, you are no fun to be with. But when you have had ample rest, you will have a more positive outlook; you will be eager to move through the day; you'll make better judgments and decisions.

Don't overlook the simplest and easiest way to get healthy. Get some sleep! If not for yourself, then do it for the people who have to live with you. (And if those reasons aren't enough, then do it so you'll have enough mental clarity to resist the sales pitch on that infomercial for the cellophane body wrap that supposedly burns your fat away while you sleep.)

# Stuff

*We must look on all things of this world
as none of ours, and not desire them.*
CLEMENT OF ROME

We don't know you very well, but we suspect that ever since you were little, you've been collecting stuff. By the time you were three years old you probably had an impressive collection of stuffed animals, toys, games, and a favorite blanket or two. From that time until now—with the help of your family and friends—you have probably collected (and discarded) enough stuff to fill a warehouse. And you're just getting started! Before long you will have a serious space problem because of all your stuff.

We'll let you figure out your storage needs, but we would like to comment on the stuff itself. First of all, allow us to define what *stuff* is in the first place. Essentially, stuff is material. Whether we're talking about stuffed animals, action figures, video games, clothing, jewelry, electronics, furniture, cars, or even houses, it has all been made or manufactured from raw materials.

Depending on the design and the quality, some of these things can be very beautiful, so beautiful that we think they enhance us or give us prestige. Other things can be highly functional and useful to our lives, so that we wonder how we ever got along without them. And still other things are of no value to other people, but they have great sentimental value to us, because they remind us of certain important people or events.

When things fall into the category of beautiful, functional, or sentimental, it's very easy to get attached to them. So attached that we lose perspective and think that we would never be the same without those things. It's okay to value certain objects, but remember that things—no matter how valuable—can be lost, stolen, or destroyed. By the same token, things can be replaced.

What can't be replaced are people and relationships. This may sound a little trite, and it may fall into the category of "Well, that is obvious," but we want to make this point because we see too many people, too many couples, and too many families living under the control of material things. They work hard so they can have nice things, but then the nice things take charge of their lives; and then they end up working *for* the things. The last thing you want to do is be caught up in the endless cycle of payments and interest charges as you pay for all your stuff. You don't want the stress and worry associated with such a condition.

And even if you are fortunate enough to never have to worry about money, the accumulation of wealth can be just as big a problem as the lack of wealth. Materialism in any form, whether you have a lot or a little, can interfere with your relationships, especially your relationship to God.

To keep your life in perspective, keep all your stuff in perspective. It's a simple matter, but oh so important.

# Diligence

*Nothing in the world can take the place of persistence.*
*Talent will not; nothing is more common than*
*unsuccessful men with talent. Genius will not;*
*unrewarded genius is almost a proverb.*
*Education will not; the world is full of educated derelicts.*
*Persistence and determination alone are omnipotent.*
*The slogan "Press On" has solved, and will solve,*
*the problems of the human race.*
CALVIN COOLIDGE

*We* don't know the specifics of your life, but we know that you've got some projects that you are working on. We aren't talking about refinishing that antique dresser you purchased at a garage sale last summer, and we don't mean your constant struggle to lose five pounds of unwanted body weight (that seem to reappear every Monday morning). Instead, we are referring to those major undertakings in life that are the focus of your time and energy over long periods. Maybe you are going to night school to obtain a college degree. Maybe you are working diligently to get yourself out of debt. Maybe you are trying to acquire new skills that will qualify you for a promotion at work. Whatever it is, you are to be congratulated for your initiative.

Sometimes getting started on a major life-changing project is the easiest part. Sticking with it can be the hard part. A certain excitement comes with your initial progress, but after an extended time of seeing only modest results, you may be tempted to pack it up and abandon the project. Don't let that happen to you. Stay with it.

The difference between success and failure in life is often just a simple matter of diligence. Diligence is nothing more than perseverance—sticking with something until you have reached your goal. Your continued effort now will result in privilege later.

Diligence will bring you success that will separate you from people who are mediocre. Unfortunately, mediocrity is much easier to obtain. Here are five steps to achieving mediocrity:

❶ Only do the minimum that is required.

❷ Wait until the last minute.

❸ Be unprepared.

❹ Accept mistakes and errors as a fact of life.

❺ Let someone else do it.

Your diligence will set you apart from those who find mediocrity acceptable. Hang in there. Be willing to do today what others will not, so you can do tomorrow what others cannot.

# Goals

*Don't let anyone think less of you
because you are young.
Be an example to all believers in what you teach,
in the way you live, in your love,
your faith, and your purity.*

1 TIMOTHY 4:12

*Unless* you are as motivated as the third monkey running up the ramp to Noah's ark, you may want to set a few goals to give your life some direction. You don't have to be young to set some goals for your life; goals are appropriate at any age. And you don't have to wait until January 1$^{ST}$ because every goal doesn't have to be a New Year's resolution. Take a few minutes, right now, to think about setting some goals for yourself.

Goals can be applied to all areas of your life: spiritual, mental, social, financial, physical, and so on. Knowing where you want to go is important—but you also need to know how to get started. Here are a few guidelines that might help:

❶ *Your goals should be in writing.* Keeping them in your head isn't very effective. You need to put them on paper so you can review them.

❷ *Your goals should be specific and measurable.* Set a goal that lets you check your progress. For instance, "Get to know God better" is admirable, but it is not a well-defined goal. A better-stated goal might be to read through the New Testament during the year, or to have a daily prayer time.

❸ *Your goals should be ambitiously obtainable.* If you make them too easy, then they will be meaningless. If you make them impossible to obtain, then they will be discouraging.

❹ *Your goals should be accompanied by an action plan.* Suppose you have a goal to lose ten pounds (okay, fifteen); you've got to have a strategy for doing it (like exercising more often than once a millennium).

❺ *Your goals should be reviewed.* Check your progress periodically to see how you are doing. You may have to adjust your goals or the action plan to keep on course.

It is much easier to get some place in life if you are making plans on how to get there.

# Success

*"Be strong and courageous, and do the work.*
*Don't be afraid or discouraged by the size of the task,*
*for the LORD God, my God, is with you.*
*He will not fail you or forsake you."*

1 CHRONICLES 28:20

*Our* society worships success. The shelves at Borders and Barnes & Noble are filled with books telling you how to obtain it. If you watch much late-night television, you are bound to see some testimonials by people who have supposedly obtained it (and to find out more, you can order a videotape for only three monthly installments of $19.95). The magazines at the grocery store checkout line have successful people on the covers. Unfortunately, society's obsession with money and celebrity status has tainted the definition of success. If you believe the magazine covers, the only people who are successful are the rich and famous. But true success isn't about wealth or notoriety.

Real success is the simple matter of progressive accomplishments in your life and your character.

There is a big difference between what you own and who you are. You are not defined by your acquisitions; the real you is revealed by your character. This distinction is significant because it determines how you define and measure success.

Many people make the mistake of defining success by their accomplishments, or their awards, or their bank balance. Don't ever define success by such terms. Instead, view "success" as the journey you take on the way to reaching your goals. Success is not the destination; it is the daily progress you make in small steps toward that destination. "Success" is the hard work that propels you in the direction of your worthwhile goals.

Enjoy a sense of satisfaction as you work diligently on a daily basis to achieve your goals. If you are growing closer to God, that is success. If you are becoming more skilled in your career, that is success. If you are developing strong friendships, that is success. These are worthwhile goals, so the pursuit of them is success in itself.

Your enjoyment of your accomplishments and possessions will only last for a moment. The kind of person you are lasts a lifetime. Your picture may never make it to the cover of *People* or *Time* magazine. But a cover shot isn't the true measure of success.

Those magazines at the checkout line will be discarded next week, but you'll be looking at your reflection in the mirror for the rest of your life. Remember that the next time you are thinking about success.

# Going Home

*Don't let the excitement of youth
cause you to forget your Creator.
Honor him in your youth before you grow old.*

ECCLESIASTES 12:1

*We* just read a statistic in the newspaper. It said that 70 percent of the people who leave their state for college don't return home after graduation. How about you? Did you leave your home state for college? And did you stay away, or have you moved back to the town where you grew up?

If you're like most people, then the place where you live now is far from the place you used to call home. That's not a bad thing. In this day and age, it's almost expected. What isn't so good is losing the connection between the person you are now and the place where you learned those early lessons about life, relationships, and knowing God.

You know the place we're talking about. It may not be the house or even the town you grew up in, but there is a place where family and friends know you better than anyone else. They know the good parts about you, and they know your flaws. And no matter how long you've been away, they're always ready to treat you as if you never left.

If you don't appreciate this place just yet, you will soon enough. Just don't wait too long to make the connection once again. It doesn't matter if you return as a huge success or a miserable failure. The people who truly know and love you don't care about such external things. All they want to see is the real you—the you with nothing to prove and nothing to hide.

Everything we've said about home applies to someone else who knows you and loves you in spite of your successes and failures. In fact, He knows you best of all, and He loves you most of all. We're talking about God, of course, the all-powerful, all-knowing, all-everything Creator of the universe. Far from being a distant, detached force, God is a personal presence who is more like home than anything you could ever imagine.

You may not be able to go to your hometown whenever you feel like it and visit the people you love. But you can instantly have an intimate connection with the God who loves you. All you have to do is open the Bible and read what God has to say. And when you need to talk to someone, just open your heart and tell God what you have to say. It seems like such a simple matter, but the results are profound.

Just like you shouldn't wait until you're retired to visit your hometown, don't wait until you are through with life to connect with God. Don't save God for a crisis. Read what's in His Word, and tell Him what's in your heart. Do it now before another day passes.

# *E f f o r t*

*So make every effort to apply the benefits of
these promises to your life.*

2 PETER 1:5

*Anytime* you're clearly struggling with something—
whether it's academics, sports, or your job—people are
often quick to ask: "How much effort are you putting into
it?" The person who poses this question may have good
intentions, but we wonder if that's the right question to
ask. You see, *effort* is the same as *trying hard.* It's using your
energy and strength to do something, whether it's physical, mental, or even emotional.

We don't doubt for one minute that you put effort
into the important stuff of your life. When faced with a
challenge, you may not *appear* on the outside to be trying
hard (the veins in your neck aren't bulging and sweat beads
aren't forming on your brow), but when it counts you will
muster the energy and put in the time to get done what

needs to get done.

When you think about it, it's almost mandatory to put effort into things like academics, sports, or your career. You want to get a good grade, you want to improve your score, and you'd like that promotion at work. So you put in the time and effort to do well, because you know there will be some kind of reward at the end of the process.

But what if the reward—or in some cases the lack of a reward—wasn't immediate? What if you knew that no matter how much effort you put in now, you wouldn't get a reward for several years, or maybe not at all? Would you be as motivated to give it your best, or would you have a tendency to let it slide, or perhaps do nothing at all?

It's human nature to put a great deal of effort into those things with an immediate reward (or deadline), and very often we put little or no effort into those things where the reward is so far out there that we can't even see it. But it isn't always the best way to go.

Years ago, Charles Hummel wrote a little book called *Tyranny of the Urgent.* Isn't that a great title? You really don't even have to read the book to figure out the theme (although you should read it). Basically, *Tyranny of the Urgent* says that the urgent things in life will always get our attention and effort, while the things that aren't urgent will always be set aside for another day. Yet it is those *nonurgent* things that are very often the *most important.*

Have you ever thought about your relationship with God as being one of those nonurgent but very important things? It's true! You know that you should be making God your top priority, but it's so easy to submit to the tyranny of the urgent. You put your effort into those things that scream out for your attention because there are immediate rewards if you do them and immediate consequences if you don't.

But what's more important than God? What has more value, both here and in the future, than your relationship with Him? Even though there may not be a reward *now* for the effort you put into your relationship with God, He has promised an eternal reward for those who seek Him (Jeremiah 29:11–13). Not only that, but your life *here and now* will be much more peaceful, powerful, and pleasing to God.

We have found that a little effort helps when it comes to growing as a Christian. Spiritual progress won't happen by sticking a Bible under your pillow at night. (It just gives you a stiff neck.) You need to spend time in God's Word, you need to take time to pray, and you need to be around other Christians on a regular basis so you can worship Him together.

So, the next time you feel the need to put effort into something urgent, think about putting just as much effort into something important, such as your relationship with God. It will satisfy you more than you'll ever know and please God in the process.

## Failure

*Many of life's failures are people who did not realize how close they were to success when they gave up.*

$Quickly$, answer this question: Is *failure* a good thing or a bad thing?

For most people in our culture, *failure* has a negative connotation. This perception is understandable. Nobody wants to *be* a failure because in our society that means you are a loser. People mistakenly assume, however, that experiencing failure makes you become a failure. They equate the verb with the noun. (In other words, failing means you are a failure.) Nothing could be further from the truth. You aren't a failure simply because you fail at something you attempt. The act of failing doesn't make you a failure. Whether you are a success or a failure is determined by how you respond after you fail.

Failure isn't fatal. Your life doesn't end when you don't get a desired result. Your future isn't ruined just because something didn't turn out the way you wanted. You are not a loser if something goes wrong.

We aren't so naïve as to believe that all failures are inconsequential. We admit that some failures can seem like monumental catastrophes in your life. Maybe you made a colossal mistake at work and were fired. Or maybe you invested your entire retirement account in Pets.com. We aren't denying that such circumstances are tough. But mistakes like that don't make you a failure; they do, however, present you with a choice: You can call it quits and give up on life, or you can get back up on your feet and take a proactive approach to life. The choice is yours to make, and the approach that you choose determines whether you are a success or a failure.

Some people are so afraid of failure that they refrain from ever attempting something they haven't done before. They don't apply for that better position; they refuse to participate in an athletic competition; they won't attempt a new hobby. They are afraid to fail, so they don't even try. How ironic! Their fear of failure prevents them from engaging in new and different experiences. They don't realize that Webster (the dictionary guy, not the little kid from the 1980s sitcom) defines *failure* as the neglect or omission to do something. Their perspective of failure is backward. Instead of viewing failure as an unsuccessful attempt, they should realize that they become a failure if they refuse the attempt simply because it may not succeed. The greatest failure is the failure to try.

You can put a positive spin on any failure that occurs in your life. You can turn what seems to be a bad thing into a beneficial opportunity. It is just a simple matter of making a choice to learn from a mistake and start anew. Don't regret the fact that your attempt failed. Take pride in yourself because you made the attempt.

# Problem Solving

*Dear brothers and sisters,*
*whenever trouble comes your way,*
*let it be an opportunity for joy.*

JAMES 1:2

*Life* is full of problems. It's guaranteed. But those problems don't have to get the best of you. There is a way to solve them. Better yet, there is a way to actually enjoy your problems.

We're not trying to put a happy spin on the troubles that come your way from time to time. Happiness is a temporary emotional feeling. Joy, on the other hand, is a deep, abiding confidence that God is in control, no matter what happens. Now, that doesn't mean that you don't get involved in solving your problems. God doesn't expect you to "sit back and relax" as He works everything out. Neither should you try to avoid problems. You need to face your problems by taking steps to solve them, as long as you trust God for the results.

The first thing you need to know is this: Problems generally fall into one of three categories—people, goals, and God. Despite your best efforts to get along with *people*, there will always be those who aggravate you. No matter how hard you work to achieve your *goals*, you will run into challenges along the way. And just when you think you are closest to *God*, temptation will rise up to meet you. Let's take a look at these one at a time.

## PEOPLE

The best way to handle your people problems is to *prepare*. Rather than being surprised at the way people treat you, get to know people and what makes them tick. In other words, become a student of human nature. People are very predictable in the way they act. (That includes you, by the way.) The more you understand personality styles, the less you will be surprised by the different ways people treat you or react to you.

Preparation isn't just about knowing people. It involves loving people as well. We're not talking about love based on feelings, but rather love rooted in the love God has for you. "Dear friends, since God loved us that much," the apostle John wrote, "we surely ought to love each other" (1 John 4:11). This kind of love doesn't come naturally or easily. You must get ready to love the people you live with and work with and meet each day by thinking about the ways God loves you.

## GOALS

What do you do if you run into challenges in the pursuit of a goal? The best advice we can give you is to *persevere*. The great English writer Samuel Johnson said, "Great works are performed not by strength but by perseverance." A lot of people try to overcome their obstacles by sheer talent or the irresistible nature of their personality. Your gifts and your charisma may get you started on a goal, but you need perseverance to finish.

The truth is that anything worth doing has its share of problems. But in the midst of problems is when you get really good at something. That's when you grow in your profession, your relationships, and in your character. "For when your faith is tested, your endurance has a chance to grow," the Bible says. "So let it grow, for when your endurance is fully developed, you will be strong in character and ready for anything" (James 1:3).

### GOD

We'd all like to believe that a personal relationship with God is like a walk in the park, but it's much more challenging than that. The problem is that we are tempted to put other things in God's place, even good things. God doesn't cry out for our attention, but our own desires certainly do.

When you are tempted by the desire to disobey God (or simply ignore Him), the best advice we can offer is to *pray.* First of all, pray that God will help keep you from temptation. When temptation does come, pray for the strength to avoid caving in. And if you do cave in, pray and ask God to forgive you, effectively eliminating all kinds of problems down the road.

*Prepare, persevere, pray.* Three powerful ways to solve the problems that come your way.

# Initiative

*Some people dream of worthy accomplishments.*
*Other people wake up and work hard to achieve them.*
*The difference is initiative.*

*Everyone* wants to accomplish something. Finishing a project gives you a sense of self-worth. Whether it is cleaning the garage, redecorating the kids' bedrooms, or organizing a charity banquet, you'll feel better about yourself when the job is finished.

*Finishing* is usually the fun part. *Starting* is usually the hardest part. That's where most of us encounter difficulty. We have a tough time getting started. There are always plenty of excuses or distractions that cause us to postpone getting started. But there is a solution. It is a simple matter of initiative.

Initiative is more than the act of doing something that needs to be done. Initiative prompts you to tackle the task before you are told, before you are asked, and before the last minute. For example, good employees do what they are asked to do. Great employees see what needs to be done and do it before they are asked. Initiative makes the difference. Similarly, initiative can make a person a better friend, spouse, or parent.

Remember that famous slogan "Just do it"? Well, with the tasks, projects, and responsibilities of life, that motto is applied differently depending on one's character:

The sluggard says: "I'll do it later."

The average person says: "I'll do it before it's due."

But the person with initiative says: "I'll do it now."

How can you tell whether or not you have initiative? Here's an easy test: How do you feel about your alarm clock? Is it your friend or your enemy? The person with initiative wants to: get up, go out, and work on. Without initiative, it's simply: lie down, stay in, and goof off.

We recognize that your schedule may be jam-packed with activities. Perhaps you are already so busy with the projects you've taken on that you haven't got a spare second to meditate on the subject of initiative. If that's the case, then "getting started" isn't your problem, and you are to be congratulated on mastering the simple matter of initiative. (Although you don't struggle with initiative, you might have the opposite problem—the inability to say "no" when people ask for your help. So, before you dislocate your shoulder from patting yourself on the back for your outstanding initiative, read the next chapter.)

# Commitments

*Do not mistake activity for achievement.*

*All* of us desire to be liked. And there is nothing wrong with wanting people to be friendly toward you. But attempting to please everyone can be dangerous. You run the risk of saying "yes" to everyone who asks for your help.

Don't get us wrong. We aren't suggesting that you become an ogre and snarl at anyone who requests your assistance. But you need to guard yourself from becoming overcommitted.

If you make a commitment to do something, then your integrity and reputation are on the line. You should work diligently to fulfill your promise. Finish the project on time, and do a quality job. That won't happen if you have made so many other promises and commitments that your "to do" list exceeds the memory capacity in your handheld computer.

If you are overcommitted, you probably lack the ability to say "no." Perhaps you don't want to disappoint each friend who makes a request of you, so you agree to accept additional responsibilities (while at the same time you are wondering where you will find the time and the energy to accomplish those projects). But you aren't doing your friends any favors if your busy schedule forces you to miss the deadlines or do a slipshod job. If that is likely to happen, then you will be doing your friend a favor if you decline the request.

Overcommitting yourself isn't fair to all of the people who are relying on your promises. It also isn't fair to the members of your immediate family and your closest friends. When you spread yourself too thin, you are in crisis mode all of the time. Everything is an emergency. You are always running behind schedule. You have no leisure time, and everything you do is rushed. That is no way to live. (If your family and friends haven't told you so already, we can guarantee you that they are thinking it.)

If you are serious about your commitments, you won't take on more than you can handle. It is a simple matter of knowing when to say "no."

# Perspective

*It isn't your position that makes you happy or unhappy.*
*It is your disposition.*

*In* the twelfth century, two bricklayers were working on the Notre Dame project in Paris. A bystander asked, "What are you doing?" One of the workers responded sarcastically, "What does it look like I am doing? I'm laying bricks!" The other bricklayer, who had a totally different perspective about his labor, answered the bystander's question with this response, "I'm building a beautiful cathedral."

In the midst of all your hard work and the hectic pace of your busy schedule, it is important for you to maintain your perspective. This is a simple yet essential technique for maintaining your sanity. You might be tempted to consider that your activities are meaningless or mundane, and perhaps that's true if you've disconnected them from the important aspects of your life. But don't look at your tasks as isolated actions. Instead, see them as part of the larger purpose of your life. When viewed in that context, they are connected in some way to your relationships with your family and friends. Your job isn't meaningless labor if you view it as the means by which you provide financially for your family. The household chores aren't as mundane when you see them as part of what it takes to create a nice environment for those in your home. Each activity is like a brick you are laying to build the cathedral that is your life.

Perspective: It is a simple matter of looking at the little things and seeing the big picture.

# Creativity

*Creativity is not dulled by age, only by disuse.*
O. ALDRICH WAKEFORD

*At* the risk of offending every schoolteacher and college professor, we would like to express this humble (but correct) opinion: Creativity and imagination are more valuable than knowledge. There! We said it. Now, allow us to quickly explain (and defend) that opinion before we are sued by some teachers' union.

Knowledge can be acquired. It can be looked up in a book. If you don't have it, you can find it. There is plenty of it available. Creativity and imagination, however, aren't as plentiful. Every person has a degree of creativity and imagination, but those qualities have to be nurtured. They aren't acquired simply by reading an encyclopedia.

Knowledge is an important aspect of life. Without it, you might end up in jail or in the hospital (depending on whether you lacked knowledge about the criminal laws or the law of gravity). But mere knowledge tends to be rather sterile and unrewarding. Creativity and imagination, on the other hand, will bring excitement and variety into your life. With knowledge, you will have an existence; with creativity and imagination, you will have a life.

Develop your God-given creativity and imagination. Look for opportunities where you can put those qualities to their fullest advantage. You will enjoy the experience. And everyone around you will appreciate the results. People with knowledge are as common as commercials during a Super Bowl telecast. But people with creativity and imagination are a rare and valuable commodity.

You can quickly dispel boredom and monotony from your life. It is a simple matter of expressing the creativity and imagination that are within you.

# Tomorrow

*I have no greater joy than to hear
that my children are walking in the truth.*

3 JOHN 4 NIV

*Regardless* of whether you have just stepped on the path of life or whether you have been walking on it for many decades, you have more walking to do tomorrow. Because the length and terrain of the path ahead are big unknowns for everyone, people often ponder this question: "What is going to happen next in my life?"

Of course, everyone deals with this question in a personal way. A few people seem to have an unwavering sense of direction in life that allows them to dismiss this question without much thought. The rest of us struggle and wrestle with this question; we are desperate to know what lies just ahead on the path. But all of our anxiety is futile. When we strain to see what's up ahead, we just end up with the same uncertainty—and a headache from squinting.

Don't be envious of those few people you know who seem to be at peace with tomorrow's unknowns. You can be glad for them. In fact, try to achieve that same tranquility in your own life. All you have to do is walk into the future one day at a time.

The rest of your life will have a few twists and turns, and you'll never be able to see beyond the next bend. God doesn't give you a map—but you can take comfort in knowing He has seen where the road ends, and He knows every curve along the way. If He thinks that the terrain ahead is too tough, He will handle the necessary road repairs before your arrival.

Always remember that your future is not dictated by your present circumstances. God can direct the circumstances of your life in lots of ways. Make reasonable plans for the future. But don't get an ulcer in the planning process.

As you consider what may happen tomorrow, don't think so much about what you will be doing. Instead, concentrate on the type of person you will become. It is not the nature of your activities that matters; it's the kind of person you are that counts. You never get to a point where you have achieved perfection. Regardless of your current age, you should keep working on becoming a better person.

What you end up doing is not nearly as important as who you end up being.

When life is over, all of a person's fame and fortune can be reduced to a file folder in some probate lawyer's office. (Just ask Bruce. He has an entire file room stuffed with probate files.) A probate file may give you some detailed information about a person's vital statistics (such as the date of birth, date of death, and a Social Security number), but there is something that is never adequately reflected in the lawyer's file. . .the quality of the person's character.

As you take aim at tomorrow, pick a worthy target. Make sure you are headed toward things that matter. Focus on things like these:

enthusiasm for life;

kindness and sensitivity;

integrity and virtue; and most important

love for God.

Ironically, "tomorrow" never comes, because with each new day there is always another "tomorrow." So, in a very real sense, you are always heading toward tomorrow. Each day involves the process of walking into the next day. Make sure you are walking in the right direction (and don't forget to enjoy the journey).

# RELATIONSHIPS

*Relationships are
all about love.*

# Friendship

*There are "friends" who destroy each other,*
*but a real friend sticks closer than a brother.*
PROVERBS 18:24

Some people make friends easily. For the rest of us, friendships are harder to establish.

Many of your friendships will begin in the context of social situations. You will see these people at work, or in the neighborhood, or at church. Most of these individuals will be "casual" friends. They are nice and you will enjoy their company, but you may not have a desire to know them much better. Most casual friendships stay that way, because they are based on a few things that you have in common (like where you work, where you live, or where you worship).

Casual friendships are great, but close friendships are better. These will be the casual friends you'll want to know better. You will intentionally start spending more time together. That's how meaningful friendships begin. . . slowly.

You'll have a lot in common with the people who become your closest friends, but it won't be "things" as much as it is "beliefs." You will share similar commitments in faith, character, and integrity.

The people who become your closest friends probably won't be exactly like you. After all, you are one of a kind. You will come to appreciate each other's similarities, but you will admire each other's differences.

You will find an interesting distinction between your casual friends and your closest friends. The casual friends will be around whenever they need you. Your closest friends will be around whenever you need them.

Close friendships have certain characteristics that aren't found in casual friendships:

❶ *Close friends accept each other.* If you spend too much time with your casual friends, each of you will become irritated and annoyed by the other person's peculiarities and idiosyncrasies. That won't happen with your close friends. Those differences won't divide you.

❷ *Close friends encourage each other.* Close friends have a kind of power over each other. This isn't a manipulative power. It is an uplifting power that allows you to build each other up. The comment from a casual friend won't do much to cheer you if you are feeling depressed, but a word of encouragement from a close friend will be very comforting.

❸ *Close friends forgive each other.* If you are like most people, your natural reaction is to hold a grudge when someone offends you. (You know you shouldn't, but you actually enjoy that feeling of righteous indignation.) But best friends don't treat each other like that. They don't want to hold a grudge against each other because it interferes with the relationship. They are quick to forgive each other. This is easy to do because you firmly believe that your close friend would never do anything to intentionally offend you.

❹ *Close friends sacrifice for each other.* Shallow and casual friendships fall apart in the midst of a crisis. When the going gets tough, immature friendships evaporate. But the opposite is true with close friendships. Tough times strengthen a close friendship because the bond of commitment to each is revealed.

Difficult circumstances usually give one friend the opportunity to act sacrificially for the sake of the other. True friends don't consider themselves "too important" to help. There is no price "too high" to pay for the sake of your true friend.

True friendship is mostly a matter of love. It comes from each of you wanting what's best for your friend more than for yourself. It is recognizing that God is working in your life through your friend, and He is using you in this same way in his or her life as well. When that type of mutual commitment exists, a bond of loyalty is forged. A paraphrase of 1 Corinthians 13:7 says it this way:

> *If you love your friend, you will be loyal to that friend no matter what the cost. You will believe in that friend when others are skeptical; you will always expect the best of that friend when others criticize; and you will always stand your ground in defending that friend when others gossip.*

Isn't that just the kind of friend that you want to have? Isn't it the kind of friend you want to be?

# Caring

*The first duty of love is to listen.*
PAUL TILLICH

*In* order for people in a civilized society to get along, people have to be civil. (Basically, that means people have to be polite.) Civility is necessary, but it's not terribly personal. That's where *courtesy* and *consideration* come in. When you display good manners, you're being *courteous*. To be *considerate* of someone means that you are aware of that person's feelings and needs. Both qualities are extensions of civility. They are how you get along and function with people in an orderly manner.

As important as civility, courtesy, and consideration are, they don't go far enough. Simply being polite or eating with a napkin in your lap isn't going to build any kind of personal relationship with anybody. If you want to get to know people on a meaningful level, not only must you be aware of their needs, but you must also be willing to do something to help meet those needs. That's what *caring* is all about. Caring takes consideration to another level. It goes beyond courtesy. Caring means being truly concerned for others. It means putting their interests above your own.

A lot of us have a natural tendency to evaluate people before we decide we want to care for them. (Okay, we'll be honest—*we* have a natural tendency to do this, and it's called *judging*.) Oh, we'll be courteous and considerate, but before we get to the level of caring, we qualify others first, as if they have to meet some kind of external standard. By contrast, a caring person looks past the outward dimension and gets right to the heart. Rather than prejudging people before they even get to know them, caring people show genuine interest, regardless of circumstances or personality.

The simple truth is that when you sincerely care for people, you will always be a person with whom others feel comfortable. They will know that you don't have some hidden agenda. They'll be confident you won't judge them, and they'll know you will listen to them.

In fact, listening may be the biggest part of caring. You focus on the other person, smile at them as they talk to you, and you actively hear them. You literally enter into their worlds. By caring about others in this way, you demonstrate the love of God to them. You imitate Him by focusing on people individually, even when you're in a crowd. People never feel insignificant around someone who truly cares.

# Encouragement

*It is wonderful to say the right thing at the right time!*
PROVERBS 15:23

A little encouragement can make a big difference. It's such a simple matter, and it doesn't take much effort—maybe only a few words or a small act of kindness. It might not seem like much to you, but it could be everything to the person who receives it. Whenever you encourage others, you are showing that you have care and concern for them. Few things in life are so easy to give and have so much impact.

God is in the business of encouraging people, but He needs your help. He can use your arms to embrace someone who is falling. He can use your voice to speak to someone who is hurting.

Knowing how to be an encouragement to someone else can be tricky, though. Sometimes people need a word of encouragement that will challenge them. You might need to shake them up a little bit. Other times, they need a word of comfort and kindness.

The distance between a "kick in the pants" and a "pat on the back" is only a few vertebrae, but this isn't purely a matter of physiology. Instead, it has more to do with your sensitivity. You have to be sensitive about what you say, and when you say it.

Once you deliver your message of encouragement, be prepared to actually do something. Your good intentions are meaningless unless you put them into action. Don't be so worried about *how* you are going to convey a message of encouragement that you fail to do anything at all. Even a feeble attempt at encouragement is better than no attempt at all.

Pray for God's wisdom and love, and then trust your instincts. Say and do what is in your heart. You will never know how much your encouraging words may help another person. But you will know in your heart that it was the right thing to do.

# Flexibility

*I fit in with them as much as I can.*

1 CORINTHIANS 9:21

$Do$ you get frustrated when people let you down? We're not talking about major disappointments, because often it's the small matters that seem to get the best of us. For example, someone agrees to meet you at a certain time, and they don't quite make it. They're late. They keep you waiting. They lose track of time while you're watching the clock. As the minutes click by, you start to fidget. Your body language changes from a position of relaxation to total discomfort. Your eyes narrow, your back stiffens, and your lips tighten as you check your watch again and again.

Or someone promises to deliver a project at a certain time, and they don't get it done. You've held up your end of the bargain, but your friend fails to do what he or she was supposed to. So you stand there with your arms crossed and your foot tapping, waiting to hear a good excuse—

only you don't get one. It's frustrating.

At the heart of your frustration (and the physical symptoms that go with it) is a certain lack of flexibility. Flexibility is nothing more than adjusting to others' differences. It's allowing for variation and movement. It is a little different from tolerance, which has more to do with letting others be themselves. Flexibility is about adjusting your schedule or your style to accommodate the different schedules and styles of others.

Being flexible involves an element of compromise. It means you understand you won't always get your way and other people won't always follow your schedule. If you're going to accomplish your goal of getting someplace or getting something done, you may have to flex a little.

Another dimension to flexibility involves knowing which battles are worth fighting and which ones are better left alone. Sometimes you need to fight the battle because certain principles that really matter to you are in jeopardy. These are principles of the heart, principles of integrity and self-respect. But most of the time the battles aren't worth fighting. Rather than trying to force others into your schedule and style (which will just cause frustration), be flexible by giving them room to be themselves. True flexibility means you make adjustments on the outside without compromising your inner principles.

Try it—and relax.

# Ambition

*Those who yield themselves up to
the influence of ambition will soon lose themselves
in a labyrinth of perplexity.*

JOHN CALVIN

*There's* nothing that gets more in the way of healthy relationships than ambition.

Don't get us wrong. We admire ambitious people, and we have been known to be ambitious ourselves. But ambition is not a totally noble virtue. Just the opposite. If left unchecked, ambition can become an all-consuming vice that destroys nearly everything in its path.

Much of the problem lies in our way of life, especially those of us who have grown up in a culture of affluence. We are surrounded by messages that call out for us to improve ourselves, to acquire more things, to gain more knowledge, and to increase our popularity. We believe we need to expand our borders and climb the ladder so we can reach the highest place possible. We crave admiration and respect.

Only respect doesn't work that way. People may say they admire someone who has clawed his way to the top, but it's not the kind of admiration that inspires others. It's more like admiring the precise and brutal way a shark attacks its victim. You are amazed at the process, but you don't approve of the way it's done—especially if you are the victim!

Don't get caught in the trap of misguided ambition, where pride and arrogance act as the snare. Don't let the engine of your life drive you to use and abuse others rather than love and care for them. You may get ahead in the short term, but in the end the price will be greater than the reward.

On the other hand, you don't want to get caught in the trap of laziness and indifference. Just like it's easy to think too much of yourself, it's also possible to think too little. Nobody—not even your closest friend—likes it when you host pity parties for yourself and lie around in a general state of malaise. That's a sure way to repel rather than attract people.

As in most things in life, we need to aim for a balance. There's a happy medium between blind, sharklike ambition and sleepy-eyed, slothlike laziness. And the balance is found in God. In his book, *A Long Obedience in the Same Direction,* Eugene Peterson writes that we should focus on aspiration rather than ambition. That's where the balance is found. "Aspiration is the channeled, creative energy that moves us to growth in Christ, shaping goals in the Spirit," writes Peterson. "Ambition takes these same energies for growth and development and uses them to make something tawdry and cheap."

There's a sense of the divine in aspiration. To *aspire* literally means "to breathe toward." When you are ambitious, you have a desire to achieve. It's an inward, self-focused thing. But when you have aspirations, you breathe your desires outward, toward something else. You channel your gifts and energies toward God. You want to be what He wants you to be rather than what you want for yourself.

The difference is that God wants us to be people who experience and exhibit "love, joy, peace, patience, kindness, goodness, faithfulness, gentleness, and self-control" (Galatians 5:22–23). These are the qualities that build relationships rather than tear them down. By contrast, when we take things into our own hands, building relationships for our own benefit, we end up falling into "sexual immorality, impure thoughts. . .hostility, quarreling, jealousy, outbursts of anger, selfish ambition. . ." (Galatians 5:19–20).

Even though the differences are clear, the choice between ambition and aspiration isn't always easy. Laying aside our selfish ambition doesn't come naturally. We need God's help—and He is more than willing to give it. We need to turn our ambitions into aspirations and direct them to God.

# Leadership

*"In this world the kings and great men*
*order their people around. . . .*
*But among you, those who are the greatest should take*
*the lowest rank, and the leader should be like a servant."*
LUKE 22:25–26

*Life* can be difficult if your boss (or some other person who is in leadership over you) acts like an authoritarian. That approach is not uncommon. It is used by a lot of leaders (usually the immature ones). Have you ever heard anyone say "Do as I say, not as I do"? Or how about "Do what I say because I'm in charge"? Of course you have. You may have even said those things yourself to someone else.

Leadership doesn't have to be that way, though. There is a better approach.

The best leadership style (for both the leader and the followers) is "servant leadership." This is not an oxymoron (like *jumbo shrimp* or *voluntary tax*). Instead, it describes the leadership style modeled by Jesus Christ. He served His followers; He didn't boss them around. They were motivated by what He did *for* them, not by what He threatened to do *to* them.

Authoritarian leaders are interested in making themselves look good. They want to feel important, so they often humiliate people in the process.

Servant leaders, on the other hand, are more interested in their followers than in their own reputations. They accept more than their share of the blame and less than their share of the credit. They act with humility so their followers feel a sense of self-worth.

Perhaps you are currently in a situation where your boss or manager is an authoritarian. If that is your situation, then you probably can't do much to change that person's style of leadership. You may be stuck for a while (so stop searching the Internet for instructions on "tar and feathering"). Prayer will help, but you should pray for yourself more than for your leader.

When you are stuck with a difficult supervisor, you have the opportunity to exhibit leadership within your group (even though you are not "the leader"). We are not talking about a mutiny (although that may be tempting). You can influence others in the group by the way you respond to the unreasonable demands of your leader. If you respond with a servant's heart, you'll be setting an example for the others to follow. You can change the attitude of the entire group. That is the essence of true leadership. It is not a matter of title or position or authority. It is a simple matter of character, humility, and service.

# Marriage

*A man leaves his father and mother*
*and is joined to his wife,*
*and the two are united into one.*
GENESIS 2:24

*We've* been thinking a lot about marriage lately—not for us, mind you (we're both happily married)—but for our kids. (We each have a daughter and a son.) All four of our kids are "twentysomethings," which used to be the marrying age.

These days men and women are waiting a lot longer to get married. They don't seem to be in such a hurry (like we seemed to be). They are concentrating on school, travel, establishing a career, and simply making sure they are doing the right thing once they've found the right person.

Whether marriage is in your future or not, we'd like to give you a little "fatherly" advice about marriage. You never know when this stuff might come in handy. Besides, marriage may seem like such a simple matter on the surface, when in reality it's pretty complex. That's why you need to listen to good advice, as well as read everything you can about making a marriage work—forever.

We read lots of books, both for our personal benefit and also to do research for the books we write. Occasionally we come across something that is so profound and so significant that we just have to save it for a special moment and pass it on to someone like you. Not too long ago we came across a book about marriage, and we'd like to share a few thoughts with you from that book.

Actually, it wasn't a book on marriage. Rather, this was a collection of letters written by Dietrich Bonhoeffer, a German theologian who was executed in a Nazi concentration camp at the close of World War II. Bonhoeffer had been captured and imprisoned for resisting Hitler in Germany. While awaiting his execution, he wrote some letters on various topics, including marriage. Even in view of the fact that many of these letters were written to his fiancée, that's got to tell you a lot about how much Bonhoeffer valued marriage.

Evidently Bonhoeffer was counseling a couple about their marriage, and here is what he wrote: "From this point forward, it will not be your love that keeps the marriage together, but rather the marriage that keeps your love together."

Isn't that profound? What we took him to mean is that in marriage love will come and go. We don't think he meant the principle of love, but the *feeling* of love that is so strong when you know you want to spend the rest of your life with someone. As good as you feel when you fall in love, your feelings will come and go with changing circumstances, shifting moods, and difficult times. Trust us. It happens.

Sometimes your feelings will change for no apparent reason. Don't be alarmed. Keep a level head, try to work through the problem, and keep the lines of communication open. Most of all, never think about giving up. Here's where the marriage becomes an incredibly important factor.

When Bonhoeffer said that marriage would keep love together rather than the other way around, he was talking about committing yourself to your spouse, to your marriage, and to God. The idea is this: The sacrament of marriage (that means the sacred covenant) should become so important to the two people involved that nothing will be able to tear it apart. A marriage with that kind of commitment will not only keep love together, but it will help love grow.

The sad thing is that in our culture marriage has been cheapened. It has been taken off the divine pedestal where it belongs and brought down to the level of a common contract. Marriage is no longer a sacred union ordained by God, but a quaint—and in some circles antiquated—option that becomes a revolving door for many. Worse, an increasing number of couples are choosing to skip marriage altogether and simply live together in the mistaken belief that love will keep their relationship going and growing.

Part of the problem is that many people see marriage as a "fifty-fifty" proposition, where a husband and a wife create a partnership, almost like you would put together a business. The flaw in this reasoning is that a healthy and permanent marriage isn't built on each person going halfway. The way we see it—and this is from the Bible—husbands and wives are each called by God to give 100 percent.

Of course, such a commitment is nearly impossible without God. We are convinced that the only way to truly love your spouse is to love him or her with the selfless "I want the best for you" kind of love that only God can produce in your life. When you commit your life and your marriage to God, you are saying to Him, "I believe everything you said about love. And I believe that only you can help me love the way I should."

Furthermore, you believe that God loves marriage and hates divorce, because He knows how divorce tears a married couple apart. You believe that God created marriage for your benefit and enjoyment. And you believe that God will help both of you thrive as individuals and as "one flesh" as you love each other and glorify Him.

Wow, we've gotten kind of serious here, almost preachy. Didn't mean to. What we did mean was to share our passion for marriage. We hope you found it helpful.

# Pets

*The godly are concerned for the welfare of their animals.*

PROVERBS 12:10

*You* may be wondering why we're including a chapter on pets in this section on relationships. Hey, that should be obvious. Just look at how we refer to our pets. They are "part of the family" or "man's best friend." No, pets aren't like normal animals that roam the woods or provide us with food (unless you have adopted Elsie the cow). Pets are a part of our everyday lives.

If you had a special pet growing up, you can identify with what we're saying. Your pet entertained you, gave you companionship, and loved you unconditionally, even when you forgot to feed him. And if you were the one entrusted with the care and feeding of the family pet, then your pet also taught you responsibility.

You may be a special creature made by God, but so is

your pet. Even though you are set apart from the animal kingdom by virtue of the divine image God has imprinted on your DNA, you and your pet share the same Creator. As the famous poem goes:

*All things bright and beautiful,*
*All creatures great and small.*
*All things wise and wonderful,*
*The Lord God made them all.*

So be kind to animals of all kinds, especially the ones who share your roof. It seems like such a simple matter, but it's an important matter for God.

# Politics and Worldview

*If I had my time again,
I would be stronger on social injustices
and less involved in parties and politics.*

BILLY GRAHAM

*Politics* is a hot topic these days. People of all stripes get interested in politics and political parties when it's time to vote, of course, but in between elections the public interest in the political process doesn't wane a bit. If anything, we are more interested in the views of our elected officials *after* we elect them than we are before they take office, when image seems to count for more than substance.

When it comes to the substance of politics, you're going to find a direct correlation between political views and worldviews. You may not find a complete connection between a particular political view and a particular worldview, but often the similarities are striking.

You see, by definition a worldview is a system of thought through which everything is given meaning. Your worldview helps you make sense of the world. It's the filter for everything you experience in life. So whether you are a teacher, a business owner, a physician, or a politician, your worldview influences what you do.

At the risk of oversimplifying things, we're going to tell you that there are only two basic worldviews. One includes God and the other one doesn't. One worldview is rooted in *theism,* while the other has its basis in *atheism* or *naturalism.* And here's something else to consider. Simply believing in God doesn't mean you have a theistic worldview. It's possible to believe that God exists while at the same time living and acting as if He doesn't. (It's called practical atheism.)

This is often the case where politics is concerned. Professed belief in God doesn't necessarily translate to decisions that honor God. On the other hand, someone who doesn't claim to be a Christian may believe in principles that are consistent with a theistic worldview. It can get rather confusing.

That's why it's important to concentrate on your own

worldview. Learn the differences between the two major worldviews we have described. As for your political views, discover for yourself what the Bible says about our responsibility to the government and to our fellow citizens. Find out what the Bible says about the sanctity of life and the need to care for the disadvantaged.

As you study and learn, keep in mind that the Bible is not a political book; in fact, it's remarkable how far the Bible seems to stay away from politics. Instead, the Bible is a manual for life, because it was written by the One who created all things and who knows us better than anyone else. The Bible tells us how to relate to God (love Him with all of our heart, soul, mind, and strength), and it tells us how to relate to others (love our neighbor as much as we love ourselves).

Even if you don't ever develop a keen interest in politics, know your own worldview, and never forget about your responsibility to God and to others. That's where your worldview must ultimately be rooted.

# Service

*If I gave everything I have to the poor
and even sacrificed my body,
I could boast about it; but if I didn't love others,
I would be of no value whatsoever.*

I CORINTHIANS 13:3

$D$o you feel the need to serve others? We're not talking about the kind of service that involves your job, because most jobs require that you deliver service of some kind. No, the kind of service we mean is a voluntary serving of others, whether you know them or not. They could be family members, friends, or complete strangers. Service means doing the kinds of things for them that you would want them to do for you.

This kind of service meets physical needs, but it also meets emotional needs. Your service may involve providing food or short-term financial assistance. Or your service may simply be an empathetic ear for someone to talk to.

You've probably noticed that some people serve others out of obligation or a selfish need to raise their standing in the community. But that's no way to serve. True, the effect might be the same no matter what the motive—people get fed, lonely people get visited—but the cause is all wrong. Any kind of catch or ulterior motive cheapens the act of service.

Worse, it puts the people being served into a position of obligation. In a sense, they become servants to the twisted emotional needs of the person doing the serving. It's all backward.

There's only one motive that makes the service you deliver honorable and true, and that's love. And there's only one way for your service to come from a heart of love. God must be in it. No, that doesn't mean you have to deliver a sermon every time you deliver a meal to someone who's hungry. It does mean you need to take on the attitude of Jesus Christ. Even though Jesus was God, He voluntarily took the role of a servant (the Bible actually uses the word "slave"—see Philippians 2:5–7) so He could meet the needs of others to the deepest level.

When you serve, don't do it from your office or your position of influence. Don't allow your service to flow from a heart empty of God's love. Instead, let the love of Jesus be your example and your motivation. Recognize that service is all about relationships, and relationships are all about love.

# Criticism

*"Let those who have never sinned throw the first stones."*
JOHN 8:7

*All* too easily, you can slip into the habit of being critical and judgmental. It often starts innocuously when you begin to notice a few flaws in the people around you. Let's face it. There are people who are worse than you—lots of them—and identifying their faults can be pretty easy. (You might even find it a little entertaining.) But there is a real danger in allowing yourself to be critical and judgmental of others. Soon you might mistakenly believe that you have value as a person while they are worthless.

When you are hypercritical of other people, you tend to exaggerate their faults while excusing or ignoring your own. You lose the ability to be compassionate and forgiving. You become elitist and intolerant. In short, you become a snob.

If you are guilty of being judgmental of others, your situation isn't hopeless. You can be reformed without shock therapy. Changing your attitude is a simple matter of honest self-examination. If you take a good look at yourself, you'll find plenty of opportunity for self-improvement. By working on making yourself a better person, you'll lose that arrogant and superior attitude. Other people will find you more enjoyable—and so will you.

# Cooperation

*It is difficult for people of different nations
to work shoulder to shoulder
when they carry a chip on one shoulder
and a gun on the other.*

*If* anything is going to get done, somebody has to do it. If you can handle the task by yourself, then there are no disputes over who is in charge or who does what. Most of the time, however, you won't be working by yourself. Many projects involve a team, and that requires some sort of working relationship among the participants. At your job, you have coworkers to contend with, while at home, other members of your family are involved. Whether you are at the office or in your living room, if more than one person is involved on a project, you've got to achieve cooperation if the job is going to get done.

Whenever two or more people are working on a project, issues of authority and responsibility are going to arise.

*Authority* usually refers to one person's power to direct the activities of the other people on the team. *Responsibility* usually refers to a person's duty to accomplish certain aspects of the job.

Many people crave authority and avoid responsibility. These individuals are more interested in *directing* the work than *doing* the work. Ironically, the people who are interested only in authority usually never get it; or, if they have it for a while, it is taken away from them because they abuse it. The person who joins a team and is anxious to receive responsibility is all too rare. Not surprisingly, those who are willing to assume responsibility usually get it.

If you are in charge of forming a team, or are assigned to one, remember that your group's success depends on cooperation. And cooperation is a simple matter if each participant is more concerned about his or her responsibility than about who has authority.

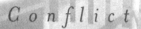

# Conflict

*"Love your enemies! Pray for those who persecute you!"*
MATTHEW 5:44

*Unless* you live alone on a deserted island or hibernate in a cabin in the Yukon, the activities of your life probably connect you with lots of other people. We aren't talking about the people driving alongside of you on the freeway during rush hour (with whom you never speak), or even the people standing only a few inches away from your face on the subway (with whom you never make eye contact). We are referring to those people with whom you interact on a daily basis. These are the members of your family, the folks in your neighborhood, and the other people at work.

Life would be much more enjoyable if you were on a friendly basis with everyone in your network of daily contacts. But that isn't real life. We just know that you are bound to have a personality clash with a few people. (We aren't saying that because we think you have an abrasive personality. We're assuming that those other people have personality flaws that cause the friction.)

Unless you can find some way to peacefully coexist, personality clashes can quickly escalate. They begin with tension and a strained relationship. If those feelings go unchecked, hostility starts to build up. Before you know it, you're immersed in full-fledged conflict. The usual consequence involves vicious gossip, playing "dirty tricks," or just acting in any manner that will annoy the other person. (If the relationship has gotten to this stage, you probably aren't faultless any longer. You can only pin some of the blame on your opponent. Your own personality and attitude have probably shifted from angelic to annoying.)

The problem is not going to get better by continuing to escalate the conflict. You may be tempted to focus all of your creativity and imagination on ways to make your adversary's life more miserable. But that won't solve your problem. Even if you end up being the conqueror, you won't feel any better. The best solution for resolving conflict and restoring tranquility in your life is to practice simple courtesy and kindness.

All of us have a natural tendency to be kind to those we like and to be hostile to those who oppose us. Feuds and wars are started because people follow these natural instincts. If you want to resolve a conflict with someone, you must resist your natural inclinations. Do the opposite: Show kindness to those who are your enemies.

Few people are willing to walk away from a fight. In our culture it is often viewed as a sign of weakness. We don't want to be labeled a coward or a sissy, so we stay engaged in the battle. After all, we think we have the right to retaliate. We want to stand up for our rights; we want to get even; we want to settle the score. But refusing to fight—and taking the additional step of extending kindness to your enemy—is not a display of weakness. Quite the contrary. Only a brave and strong individual can resist the urge to retaliate and act courteously in an attempt to diffuse an explosive relationship.

The next time you are engaged in a personality conflict, try a little courtesy and kindness. This simple technique will confuse and confound your enemy. And your response may change the attitude of your opponent.

It will surely change yours.

# Integrity

*The Lord hates people with twisted hearts,*
*but he delights in those who have integrity.*

PROVERBS 11:20

*Our* society seems to lack integrity. Maybe that is because people don't know what it is. We know that *you* have a deep understanding of the term, but there might be someone reading over your shoulder who doesn't have a clue about the definition of *integrity*. For that person's benefit, we will state what *you* already know:

Integrity is simply doing what you promised you would do. It is *telling* the truth and *doing* the truth.

Integrity is doing the right thing (even if no one would know that you did the wrong thing).

Integrity is accepting responsibility when you have made a mistake (especially if you could dodge the blame or shift it to someone else).

People who lack integrity probably got started making

ethical compromises on the small things. It is those little things that are really tempting—the tiny breaches of integrity that hardly seem to matter: No one may know, no one may get hurt, and you will come out looking better. But don't compromise on the small things, because if you do, you will build up a tolerance for doing the wrong thing. After a while, the wrong things won't seem so bad. Your conscience will become calloused. Then you will begin to struggle with making compromises on bigger issues. So instead, it is just easier to always do the right thing. Big or little. Private or public. Just do what is right.

Integrity always matters. If for no other reason, integrity matters because it is important to God. Beyond that, integrity keeps you the kind of person you want to live with. And that's important because you have to be with yourself for your entire life.

# KNOWING GOD

*It's impossible to love God unless you know Him.*

# Love

*Love never gives up, never loses faith, is always hopeful,*
*and endures through every circumstance.*

1 CORINTHIANS 13:7

*The* concept of love is often trivialized in our culture. Songs describe it as a passing emotion. Movies portray it as physical passion. Somewhere along the way in the midst of all of the hype, our society has forgotten the essence of true love. Love is simply absolute commitment.

Surprisingly, you can't expect to find true love from your relationships with family and friends. Sometimes those relationships produce hurt and sorrow instead of the love that you are hoping for. The best of those relationships might contain sincere attempts at love, but even the best spouse or parent or child or friend can't love you with complete, unselfish love. That is available only from God.

God's love is difficult to understand because it is so unusual. Some characteristics of His love are not found in any type of love that can be expressed by humanity. For instance. . .

❶ *God's love is unending.* He has loved you since you were born (in fact, He loved you even before you were born). And His love for you will last throughout eternity. That kind of love won't come from anyone else.

❷ *God's love is unconditional.* He loves you no matter what. Sure, there have been times (many of them) when He was disappointed in your behavior, but His love for you was never disrupted by your conduct. That is the amazing thing about God's grace. His love is unrelated to what you do (or don't do). Nothing you can do would make Him love you more. And nothing you can do would make Him love you less.

❸ *God's love is unbelievable.* You will be astounded when you first become aware of the nature of God's love for you. But as your relationship with Him grows stronger, you will realize that your initial understanding of His love was too simplistic. His love is deeper and stronger than you will ever fully appreciate. As you get to know Him better, you will continue to discover new characteristics and facets of His love. The more you know about Him, the more amazed you will be by Him. His love for you is incredible. It is incomprehensible.

Within every person is a longing to experience true love. You are no exception. But don't expect to find true love from another person. The love that someone else can offer to you will never be enough because it is imperfect. But don't despair. True love is not difficult to find. All you need to do is turn to God and accept the love He has for you.

## Faith

*But those who wait on the LORD will find new strength.*
*They will fly high on wings like eagles.*
*They will run and not grow weary.*
*They will walk and not faint.*

ISAIAH 40:31

*You* have a lot of things going on in your life, and you are naturally curious and maybe even anxious about the direction the Lord will lead you. But don't let anxiety overtake you.

This is an area in life where you will need to rely on faith. Not faith in the sense of whether you believe in God, and not faith in terms of whether you will stay committed to Him, but faith that means you can trust Him. Can you trust His direction? Can you trust His timing?

Psalm 23 says the Lord is your shepherd. Look at what this means:

*He is not your chauffeur. He doesn't take you wherever you tell Him you want to go.*

*He is not your butler. It is not His job to make sure you are comfortable every moment. He isn't going to cater to your every whim.*

*And He is not your tour guide. He doesn't tell you in advance where you will be going and what you will be doing.*

*He is your shepherd. The shepherd leads the sheep where they need to go to be fed and protected. He knows what is best for them.*

Having faith in God is more than having a belief in His existence. It is turning over control of your life to Him. This may be exactly what you want to do, but if you are still stressing out about the future, then you are holding back on God. True faith means that you can relax and rely on His timing and direction. Sheep don't have a very high anxiety level. They seem content to let the shepherd be in charge.

You may be thinking: "I am willing to go wherever and whenever He leads me. I just want to know now how it is going to turn out in the future." Well, it's not likely that the Lord is going to tell you in advance. He wants you to learn to trust Him. That is what faith is all about.

Don't be too anxious to see the next page of God's outline for your life. He'll turn the page and let you see it at exactly the right time. Just have faith. It is a simple matter of letting God be in charge.

# Grace

*Grace is love that cares and stoops and rescues.*
JOHN STOTT

*Have* you ever thought about all the different courses your life could have taken? There are so many options your family could have chosen. There are so many different choices you could have made. There are so many bad paths you could have walked.

If you have made mostly good choices up to this point in your life, then you are probably on the right path. And we think we know the reason why. God has been gracious to you.

All you have to do is look around at other families and other people who aren't doing as well. Don't get into the habit of comparing yourself to others, but it's hard not to see that many other people you know—and millions you don't know—are really struggling in life. They face unbelievable challenges and seemingly insurmountable odds.

Rather than gloating over your "good fortune" or pitying those who are "less fortunate," may we suggest that you do something else? Whenever you hear about another person or family buried beneath a heavy load of despair, or you hear about a family crushed by the anxiety of an illness, pray for that person or that family—and then thank God for His graciousness to you.

We once met a very successful person who was in the habit of chalking up such blessings to "luck." He said that if you have good health or work in a job you like or even find a prime parking space, then you are lucky. We'll credit the parking space to pure chance, but we don't believe for one second that the other good things in life come about by simple luck. Instead, we believe God is very much involved in the details of our lives. God directs all of us and answers our prayers and graciously gives us the things we need because He loves us, not because we deserve them.

In fact, that's what grace is all about. It's God giving us the things we don't deserve.

So what about the families and the individuals who pray and trust God and yet face difficulties? Is God gracious to them as well? Absolutely. God's grace doesn't operate on some sort of sliding scale whereby some of us get more grace than others. The simple matter is that God's grace begins with all of us being alive and experiencing some measure of joy in our lives.

Never forget that because we have sinned against a holy God who deserves nothing short of perfection, we don't deserve any of the good things we have. If anything, we deserve to die. But most of us don't die (at least not before our time)—and God has given us life to enjoy, even in the middle of difficulties. Even those people who turn their backs on God can have fulfilled lives and can enjoy most of the good things this world and this life have to offer.

You've got a lot of life ahead of you. By the grace of God, you have many years to go. And it's possible—in fact, it's almost guaranteed—that you are going to face some difficult times. But you will get through them as you have in the past, and you will find God's goodness and faithfulness in the middle of your challenges. That's what the grace of God is all about.

## *Your Past*

*Remember the days of long ago;*
*think about the generations past.*
*Ask your father and he will inform you.*

DEUTERONOMY 32:7

*Every* once in awhile you need to reflect on your family, especially your heritage. Like most people in America, you aren't that far removed from immigrant families who came to this country from another place. You may not be able to trace your ancestry to the Pilgrims, but you probably have some exciting and meaningful historical events in your family's past.

Somewhere along the line, one or more of your ancestors overcame significant opposition as they left the Old World and came to the New. More than you realize, their determination took courage and faith. It took courage because they ventured out on their own and moved—not just from one town to another—but from one continent to another at a time when travel was more difficult than it is today. They were seeking opportunity, a better life, and often freedom from oppression and poverty. You've got to admire their spirit. And their determination took faith because they couldn't always see the path ahead of them. All they had was the knowledge of what God had done for them in the past. They trusted that God wouldn't let them down in the future, just like He had not let them down in the past.

That faith is part of your heritage, and even though you may never have to leave everything behind in search of new opportunities, you can make that faith a part of your legacy. As the Bible says:

> *What is faith? It is the confident assurance that what we hope for is going to happen. It is the evidence of things we cannot yet see.* HEBREWS 11:1–2

# Knowing God

Do you have a personal mission statement? Most people haven't even thought about coming up with a statement of purpose for themselves, and that's understandable. Generally we think of companies or other organizations as having mission statements, and most do. But there's no reason why individuals can't do the same. In fact, we encourage you to come up with one.

It's really a very simple matter. When you have something written down that defines who you are and what it is you want to get done, you will be more fulfilled in your life. When we first started writing books, we decided we needed a mission statement. We wrote down all of the things that were important to us. And we wrote down what it was we wanted to accomplish through our writing. It didn't take us long to come up with something:

> *To communicate the truth about God correctly,*
> *clearly, and casually.*

What do you think? It's pretty simple, but we can tell you that those few words have motivated and directed us in ways we can't even measure. Because we've had direction and purpose, we haven't wandered aimlessly, wondering what kind of books we should write. It's been easy to turn down some projects and accept others because we have a personal mission statement to follow.

Don't get us wrong. We're not perfect. We've made mistakes, and we're not as far along as we'd like to be, but we're heading in the right direction. We believe that we're fulfilling our personal mission statement.

If you were to ask us for help in constructing your own mission statement, we would tell you that one thing needs to be at the heart of your statement: Get to know God better. No matter what else you include, this must come first. If you make this a priority for the rest of your life, everything else you do will fall into place. That doesn't mean you will automatically be a success in the world's eyes, but you will be successful in the eyes of God.

Here's what happens when you get to know God better: You will love Him more, because you will appreciate more and more who God is and what He wants for you. We would even put *knowing* God above *loving* God in terms of your everyday activities and long-term goals.

We're not saying that knowing God is more important than loving God, because Jesus Himself said that the most important thing we can do in our relationship with God is to love Him. However, we believe that it's impossible to love God unless you know Him. Even after you become a Christian, you don't have a natural desire to really love God. You may have a heart of gratitude for what God did for you, but even then a true spirit of love is impossible without first *knowing* what it is God did for you.

Knowing God involves more than just having information *about* God. It's one thing—and it's a good thing—to know that God is holy and all-powerful and all-knowing and eternal and infinite and all that. But you also need to know *how* God has operated in human history, what His desire is for you now, and what His plans are for the future (most of which can be found in the Bible). It's also incredibly rewarding to find out how God has worked in the lives of other people to accomplish His purposes, because there's a 100 percent chance that He wants to work in you and through you to do something very special as well.

As you get to know God a little more each day, your life will take on more meaning and you will feel more fulfilled. And as you get to know God better, you will get to know yourself better as well.

Oh, and if you happen to come up with a mission statement that you'd like to share with us, be sure to e-mail us a copy. We'd love to read it.

# Believing God

*"You know these things—now do them!*
*That is the path of blessing."*
JOHN 13:17

*You're* going to find throughout your life that most people believe in God. In fact, we just read a statistic in a magazine that something like 96 percent of all people in America believe in God. That figure astounded us until we read the article that accompanied the statistic. That near unanimous percentage includes many different religions—such as Hinduism, Islam, Judaism, Mormonism, and Christianity—all of which claim to believe in God. And then there are those who don't claim to belong to any particular religion, but still believe there's a God out there.

So who's right? Whose God is the real one? Are there many variations of God, or does everyone believe in the same God? Are we all climbing up the same mountain on different trails, destined to reach the same single peak where we will all see the same God?

These may sound like silly questions, but millions of people—make that *billions* of people—believe this is the way it goes. They believe that a God of love would never condemn anyone to hell. (By the way, the same magazine survey said that 72 percent of all people believe in heaven, while only 56 percent believe in hell.) Therefore, we're all going to make it to heaven, as long as we're climbing up the mountain by living pretty good lives.

Sometimes this reasoning is hard to refute. You may know the God of the Bible, and you may have personally accepted His offer of salvation through Jesus Christ. But how do you know that the beliefs of other people aren't equally valid, especially when they seem so sincere?

Throughout your life you're going to encounter a lot of people who will say they believe in God, but the minute you start talking about the God of the Bible, they will refuse to accept your "narrow" definition of who God is and what He expects of humankind. As our favorite theologian, R. C. Sproul, once said, there's a difference between believing *in* God and *believing* God. Simply believing that there is a God doesn't mean that you are going to do what He says. The Bible says that even the demons believe in God (James

2:19), and *they* certainly don't do what God says. On the other hand, when you *believe* God, you believe what He says and you take His words to heart.

When Jesus, who is God in human form, said "no one can come to the Father except through me" (John 14:6), He meant it. There isn't any way to have a personal relationship with God—there isn't another way to gain God's favor and secure your eternal destiny with God—except through the person and work of Jesus Christ.

People want to believe in God, but they don't want to believe Him. They don't want to do what He says. Remember this when someone calls your beliefs "narrow." There aren't many ways to God. There's only one. That's what it means to truly believe God.

# God's Will

*Trust in the LORD with all your heart;*
*do not depend on your own understanding.*
*Seek his will in all you do, and he will direct your paths.*

PROVERBS 3:5–6

*Maybe* you are asking: "How can I know God's will for my life?" That's a great question. Grappling with the question of how God wants to use you is a theologically deep concept. Although theologians and seminary professors can occupy themselves for hours discussing the aspects of God's will, you shouldn't be intimidated by the subject. As you will soon see, God's will is a relatively simple matter.

At the outset, it should be noted that God isn't trying to play tricks on you. Many people mistakenly believe that God's will always involves some sort of guessing game. But it never does. God doesn't joke around with His will. He doesn't hide His will and then sneak it around to confuse you. Learning His will isn't like that game where you guess which of the three shells is hiding the bean.

Discovering God's will is difficult for some people, though, because they think that God has only one, very specific plan for their life. They think that God has a preferred "Plan A," and if they choose wrong then they will be stuck with an inferior "Plan B" for the rest of their lives. Well, God is very creative, and in most circumstances His will is broad enough to give you lots of options.

Be encouraged by this thought: Before He created the universe, God knew the choices you would make in your lifetime. In His sovereignty, He can arrange the circumstances of your life as He wants them to coincide with the choices you will make. So you can be faced with a lot of choices, and they could all be acceptable in the context of God's will.

Your own talents and interests can give you a clue to what God wants. He probably longs for you to use the skills and abilities He has already given you. If He gave you a natural talent for writing, then He may somehow have you use that ability. On the other hand, He probably won't have you do anything in the medical field if you faint at the sight of a hypodermic needle.

God's will also takes on momentum as it progresses. You

probably won't find Him asking you to do something totally different from what He has prepared you to do. He builds on your past experiences to take you to the next step.

God wants us to find joy and fulfillment in what we do for Him. So don't think that following His will means He will ask you to be unhappy or uncomfortable. He's not going to lead you into a situation that will make you miserable.

Allow us to put this concept into very practical and relevant terms: God won't call you to be a missionary in Siberia just for the sheer torture of making you live without indoor plumbing. However, that doesn't mean you can always determine God's will by choosing the option that is most appealing to you. (Otherwise, all the missionaries would be in places like Hawaii. Somebody has to get stuck with Siberia.) God knows what you need and what is best for you. He has the perfect situation in mind for you. You might not recognize it at first, but trust Him:

> *"For I know the plans I have for you,"* says the LORD. *"They are plans for good and not for disaster, to give you a future and a hope."* JEREMIAH 29:11

Don't put yourself through too much mental anguish

trying to construe God's will to mean there is a certain place or thing or person that you must find. God's will doesn't usually work like that. Rather than a specific something, God's will is primarily a condition of your heart. God wants you to be willing to serve and follow Him. He wants you to be moldable and moveable. You should spend your time working on your relationship with God, and let Him be responsible for arranging the circumstances of your life to guide you where He wants you to be.

Prayer plays a big part in knowing God's will. Remember that prayer includes both talking to God and listening to Him. Don't expect that when you pray you will actually hear a James Earl Jones-type voice booming down from heaven with an answer. But when you enter into God's presence in prayer, He can guide your thoughts. That is all part of knowing His will.

Here is a radical thought: All that you need to know about God's will is in the Bible. Many people waste a lot of time trying to determine God's will over the insignificant details of life. We personally don't think God cares whether you choose cereal or pancakes for breakfast, and you certainly won't find a Bible verse about it. But the Bible tells us what is important to God, so those things ought to be our guidelines. Jesus summed it up this way:

> *"You must love the Lord your God with all your heart,*
> *all your soul, and all your mind. [And you are to] love*
> *your neighbor as yourself."*  MATTHEW 22:37–39

There it is! That is God's will for you.

We know what you're thinking: "It can't be as simple as that." But it is. When you boil it all down, God's will is not so much a thing, a time, a place, or a person. Instead, it is the attitude of your heart. If you are actively involved in loving Him and obeying Him, then you are doing what He desires. If we are focused on Him instead of ourselves, then God will take charge of leading us, and we just need to go with the flow.

But don't just take our word for it. God has specifically promised you that He will be responsible for guiding you if you obediently depend upon Him:

> *Trust in the LORD with all your heart; do not*
> *depend on your own understanding. Seek his will in*
> *all you do, and he will direct your paths.*
>
> PROVERBS 3:5–6

## Enthusiasm

*Whatever happens. . .*
*may the Lord give you joy.*
PHILIPPIANS 3:1

*We* are very excited about what we are going to share with you next—which is appropriate, since this chapter is about *enthusiasm*. Most people equate enthusiasm with excitement or extreme interest, and that's not a bad way to look at it. You probably get enthusiastic about certain things or events—whether it's something new, a great movie, or a vacation in Hawaii—because you're interested in them, and that interest creates excitement. You can't wait to try out your new DVD player, see that movie everyone is talking about, or dip your toes in the warm water of Waikiki Beach.

The excitement aspect of enthusiasm is great, but another dimension to enthusiasm gets more to the heart of what the word really means. When you break the word *enthusiasm* down, you essentially have two words: *en* and *theos. En* basically means *in,* and *theos,* well, that's the word for *God.* So, in essence, to be enthusiastic means to be in God. Isn't that great? Just by being enthusiastic, you are showing the world that God matters in your life.

Now, we're not saying that people who aren't enthusiastic don't have God in their lives. We've known Christians who are pessimistic and depressing to be around (but we try to avoid these people). On the other hand, we've met Christians who are incredibly enthusiastic, which is the way things should be. This doesn't mean you have to hoot and holler and pump your fist like Tiger Woods after a great shot, but it does mean that you have an inner joy and optimism.

If you know God personally, you should be the world's greatest enthusiast, because you have the greatest reason to be excited about life. After all, your past failings have been forgiven by God, you are living in the present power of God, and your future life with God is bright and certain.

Never get discouraged, even when others may resent your enthusiasm (and they will because you make them feel dull). Whatever you do—whether it's at home with your family, at school with your friends, or at work with your colleagues—may your enthusiasm fill your days and shine brightly for God.

# Simplicity

*Where there is simplicity, there is no artificiality.*
ALBERT E. DAY

*Here* are a few simple thoughts on simplicity:

❶ It's better to have a few things you highly value than a lot of things you don't care that much about.

❷ If you haven't worn or used something in a year, give it away.

❸ You can't attain simplicity unless you eliminate clutter.

❺ When you give God the "first" of everything—your time, your money, and your attention—life becomes much simpler and you become more effective.

# Compassion

*None are true saints except those who have
the true character of compassion and concern
to relieve the poor, indigent, and afflicted.*
JONATHAN EDWARDS

*This* is going to sound a little funny, but compassion is very popular right now. Maybe compassion is big news because we have so many reasons to be compassionate. All you have to do is read the headlines or watch CNN, and you can't help but see the suffering of vast numbers of people around the world or in your own community. Your heart goes out to people who are hurting, and you wonder what can be done. More personally, you wonder "What can I do?" We think we have some answers for you.

First, let's talk about what compassion really means. Very simply, compassion is about being so moved by the sorrow or hardship of another person or group of people that you want to help. You want to give money or do something to personally help the problem. Somehow you want to get involved in the effort to improve the situation.

You probably know some very compassionate people, and if you don't, there are many examples throughout history. In your lifetime, Mother Teresa stands out. She met the physical and spiritual needs of the poorest of the poor and the sickest of the sick in India for most of her life.

But the greatest example of compassion of all time was Jesus. Not only did He notice and meet the physical needs of people, but He saw their spiritual needs as well. Not only did He heal people, but He also forgave their sins. Obviously you have no way of forgiving sins, and you can't heal people either, but you can offer yourself to people in need, just like Jesus did.

You may be discouraged because you don't think you can ever do enough. That's normal. You may help one person, but there will always be someone else in need. The truth is, all the compassion in the world will never eliminate the need to be compassionate.

Jesus told His disciples, "You will always have the poor among you" (John 12:8). The cruel presence of disease guarantees that there will always be suffering, and the natural hostility of human beings insures that wars and conflict will never cease—at least not until Jesus returns to make the world right again. And then there are the natural disasters, like devastating rains and floods and earthquakes that always seem to hit places teeming with people. That's where you have suffering on a large, almost incomprehensible scale. How do you deal with that? How do you explain the enormous human suffering such disasters produce? The Bible tells us that nature itself is groaning under the weight of sin in our world. We believe this groaning literally produces natural disasters. So again, until Jesus makes the world right again, natural disasters will always be here, and they may even get worse before things get better.

So where's the balance in all of this? How can you properly express compassion? Our advice is that you choose one area and get involved on a consistent basis. Whether you feed hungry children, build shelters for the poor, or provide relief after natural disasters, get involved by supporting an organization that specializes in helping disadvantaged and displaced people. You can't be all things to all people, so choose an area that pulls at your heart most deeply. Then match that area with a reputable organization known for meeting the physical as well as the spiritual needs of people. For example, World Vision has an excellent track record of bringing relief to people and then helping them climb out of poverty. Habitat for Humanity is another outstanding organization that builds housing for people who have demonstrated responsibility but have never had an opportunity.

You should also make room in your schedule to volunteer your time on a regular basis. We met the chief of staff for a United States senator who teaches kids how to read on the weekends. We know of a lot of people who take short-term "mission trips" during their vacations to meet the physical and spiritual needs of people in various parts of the globe.

Above all, your compassion for others needs to be motivated by your knowledge that God has been compassionate to you. Whenever you have needed God's help, He has been there for you. Sometimes you didn't recognize it until after you went through your crisis, but He has always walked beside you in your pain. Most importantly, He showed you compassion by sending Jesus to die for you, even before you knew you needed a Savior.

The Bible says, "God showed his great love for us by sending Christ to die for us while we were still sinners" (Romans 5:8). It's one thing to show love and compassion to a friend or even a stranger, but God loved us while we were His enemies.

With God's help, that's the kind of attitude of compassion we need to have for others.

## Conflict

*Avoiding a fight is a mark of honor;*
*only fools insist on quarreling.*

PROVERBS 20:3

*We* sure don't like conflict, and we suspect you don't either. But conflict is a part of life. Here's our advice:

First, realize that a conflict usually originates somewhere else, so don't take it personally.

Second, rather than looking at the differences between you and the person with whom you're at odds, look for the things you have in common.

Third, if you can't resolve your conflict, ask an objective party to help you through the issues.

Finally, pray about the conflict. God is great at resolving our differences, as long as both parties are listening to Him.

# Inner Life

*The true inner life is no strange new thing;*
*it is the ancient and true worship of God,*
*the Christian life in its beauty*
*and in its own peculiar form.*

GERHARD TERSTEEGEN

*If* you're like most people, you probably spend a good deal of time on your outer appearance. For most of us, that's no small matter. It takes the better part of the early morning to scrub, swab, shave, and sweeten our bodies into a presentable form. Then there's all that maintenance throughout the day: combing, preening, washing, and applying. It never stops. And if you've made plans to go out in the evening, well, the whole process practically starts over.

The thing is, though, despite your best efforts, you can't do much to change your appearance. About all you can do is dust it off and shine it a bit.

The same goes for your basic personality. The way you are now, the way you've always been, and the way you're going to be tomorrow are all pretty much the same. You can dress up your personality when the occasion calls for it, but the person you are eventually comes through.

Like them or not, your physical and personality features come as a package when you're born. In fact, the Bible says you had these characteristics from the moment you were conceived. King David wrote in a psalm to God: "You made all the delicate, inner parts of my body and knit me together in my mother's womb" (Psalm 139:13). Science today has confirmed this truth—it's called your DNA.

Okay, so you can't do a whole lot to change the basic "you," although you can work to refine and enhance your features and personality. (Believe us, we've done a lot of refining over the years.) But there is a part of you—the *real* you— that you can change dramatically, depending on how you handle it. It's your inner life.

Gordon MacDonald first made us aware of the importance of cultivating your inner life in his book *Ordering Your Private World*. We use the word "cultivate" very deliberately, because that's the word he chose in the book. According to MacDonald, your inner life is like a garden. When you cultivate a garden—that is, when you prepare the soil, kill the weeds, plant the seeds, and water the plants—you are doing everything you can to help it grow. And chances are good that you're going to have a lovely garden.

On the other hand, if you simply scatter a few seeds around and then neglect your garden, you may get some plants and flowers, but they will likely be scrawny. Worse, you'll have a crop of weeds that will all but choke and destroy the fledgling plants.

We think you can easily make the comparison between the garden and your inner life. It is possible—and we highly advise this—to cultivate your inner life. Prepare your heart through prayer to receive the good things God has for you.

This doesn't mean that everything you take in has to be religious. After all, technically, everything in the world belongs to God. However, there is a lot of corruption out there, so you have to be selective about what you let through the gateways of your ears and eyes, because it goes from there into your mind and heart, which make up the inner life.

So be selective about what you read, watch, and listen

to. We're not trying to lecture you like your parents used to (although they had your best interests in mind). You are fully capable—and you are fully responsible—to make these decisions for yourself. All we can tell you is that what goes into your mind and heart comes out in your life.

What you are going to find is that you will have the most contentment, and you will experience the most satisfying inner peace, when your inner life is in order. As you carefully cultivate your inner garden, you will have a much clearer path to God, and your relationships with others will be more meaningful. It isn't easy, and the struggle to cultivate never ends. (Have you ever heard of a garden that doesn't require constant maintenance?) But with God's help and your own discipline, you will experience the satisfaction of a private world that is both ordered and productive.

# The Bible

*All Scripture is inspired by God
and is useful to teach us what is true
and to make us realize what is wrong in our lives.
It straightens us out and teaches us to do what is right.
It is God's way of preparing us in every way,
fully equipped for every good thing God wants us to do.*
2 TIMOTHY 3:16–17

*Many* people are intimidated by the prospect of knowing God. They just don't know how to start the process of establishing a relationship with Him. After all, God is immense and incomprehensible. How do you begin to know someone like that?

Getting to know God isn't as difficult as it may seem. It is a simple matter of reading the Bible. The Bible isn't some ancient book that is so outdated that it has no relevance to your life in the 21$^{st}$ century. No, it is old, but it isn't outdated. If you think that the Bible is just a bunch of archaic platitudes, then you need to realize that the Bible is God's personal message to you. God has something to say to you, and He is saying it in the pages of the Bible.

The verse that is quoted at the beginning of this chapter states that there are several distinct benefits to reading the Bible:

❶ *Motivation.* The writers of the Bible were inspired by God. His message is on those pages. When you read the Bible, you can literally read the words of God, the Creator of the universe who has a message for you. Isn't that enough motivation to get you reading?

❷ *Instruction.* The Bible is a handbook for learning about God. Think of it as an instruction manual. All that you need to know about God—and yourself—is contained on those pages.

❸ *Detection.* The Bible is like a mirror that can give you a very accurate reflection of your life. It helps you examine your thoughts and your actions.

❹ *Correction.* If your life is getting off course, God can

reveal that fact to you through the Bible.

❺ *Direction.* If your life seems to be adrift with no fixed foundation, you need to read the Bible. You will find verses that give you a sense of purpose and direction.

❻ *Preparation.* Life isn't easy, and God wants to prepare you for the circumstances that you will encounter. The Bible contains information and inspiration that you will need for situations at home, at work, and in your relationships with family, friends, and neighbors.

❼ *Realization.* Reading the Bible can give you the confidence that God is on your side. It is the best way to connect with God, because it reveals that God has a plan and a purpose for your life.

The Bible contains all of the answers and inspiration you need to succeed and thrive in life. But it won't do you any good if it is sitting on the shelf. Those divine principles won't penetrate your cranium by osmosis. Nor is there some secret procedure to obtaining all of that spiritual wisdom. It is just a simple matter of reading.

# Generosity

*The generous prosper and are satisfied;*
*those who refresh others will themselves be refreshed.*
PROVERBS 11:25

*No* matter how much or how little you have throughout your life, always be generous. Generosity doesn't come from pity or from obligation. Rather, a generous spirit comes from a heart that is overflowing with gratitude.

Some people are afraid to be generous because they fear they won't have enough left for themselves. This is utterly backward. "Try it!" God says about giving Him our offerings. "Let me prove it to you! Your crops will be abundant" (Malachi 3:10–11). What that says to us is this: God will bless us in ways we haven't even thought of—if only we will be generous.

## Patience

*Your heavenly Father already knows all your needs,*
*and he will give you all you need from day to day*
*if you live for him and make*
*the Kingdom of God your primary concern.*
*So don't worry about tomorrow.*

MATTHEW 6:32–34

*Are* you stressing over something that is happening in your life? Are you freaking out because there is nothing you can do about it? Are you gripped with anxiety because you have to wait to see how things turn out? If your life is unsettled by this type of nervousness, then we would like to recommend that you try something that might help: *patience.*

We know that patience is easy to recommend but difficult to obtain. After all, it is obvious that you don't have much patience to begin with (because your lack of it is the reason you are so anxious over the circumstances in your life). So, for you, it might be helpful to analyze why you lack the patience to wait for certain situations to come to their natural conclusions. Maybe it is because you don't like to be surprised by events in your life, so you want to know in advance how things will turn out. Or, maybe it is because you don't want to be unexpectedly hurt or disappointed. Perhaps you are just curious. These are certainly possibilities for your underlying anxiety, but we suspect that there is a more basic reason: You are just downright *impatient*.

Impatience is wasted emotion. It is absolutely worthless. It doesn't make things happen faster or differently. In fact, it is counterproductive because it distracts and upsets you.

Impatience about the future often ruins the enjoyment of the present. If you are stressed and distressed about the uncertainty of tomorrow, you won't be able to appreciate the beauty of your circumstances today.

The only antidote for impatience is its antonym: patience. Although many people desire to acquire patience, few actually get it. Ironically, the more you strain to obtain patience, the more you become anxious and worried about not having it. This makes you more *impatient*. Patience is illusive like that. As you become more nervous and fretful about acquiring it, the likelihood of getting it decreases.

Patience will only be available to you when you begin

to realize it has a spiritual dimension. We aren't suggesting that you will receive a large dose of patience from God the moment you ask Him for it. For some reason, God does not seem to respond when our prayers go something like this: "Dear Lord, please give me patience, AND GET IT TO ME NOW!"

The spiritual dimension of patience involves trust in God. In contrast, our impatience is the result of our pride. When we are impatient, we want something to happen before God wants us to know about it. But when we are willing to trust God completely—for the timing of the circumstances as well as for the specific result—then we feel a sense of peace about the situation. (That sensation may be a new experience for you, so we'll tell you what it is called: *patience.*)

Although we don't know you personally, we suspect that you have great things happening in your life *right now.* Don't be so impatient that you miss out on the enjoyment of them. Just realize that God wants and knows the best for your future. Let Him handle your future at His own pace.

Be patient.

# Small Matters

*The steps of the godly are directed by the LORD.*
*He delights in every detail of their lives.*

PSALM 37:23

*There* are no small matters to God. Nothing in the world or in your life is too insignificant for Him. How do we know that? What gives us such insight into something so profound? Well, we could give you examples from our own lives, but we don't want to bore you, so we'll simply point to the Bible, God's personal message to all of us.

King David, Israel's greatest monarch, wrote about God's intimate knowledge of everything we do:

> *O LORD, you have examined my heart and know*
> *everything about me. You know when I sit down or*
> *stand up. You know my every thought when far*
> *away. You chart the path ahead of me and tell me*
> *where to stop and rest. Every moment you know*

*where I am. You know what I am going to say even*
*before I say it, LORD.*          PSALM 139:1–4

Now, if you've got something to hide, knowing that
God knows all about you can be rather unsettling. But if
you are following His will, then knowing that God knows
every detail of your life can give you great comfort and
assurance.

As well as David knew God, Jesus knew Him much
better. In fact, no one knew God better than Jesus, because
Jesus was the embodiment of God in human form and
equal to God in every way. So when Jesus spoke, it was as
if God was speaking. And here's what Jesus said:

*"So I tell you, don't worry about everyday life—*
*whether you have enough food, drink, and clothes.*
*Doesn't life consist of more than food and clothing?*
*Look at the birds. They don't need to plant or har-*
*vest or put food in barns because your heavenly*
*Father feeds them. And you are far more valuable*
*to him than they are. Can all your worries add a*
*single moment to your life? Of course not."*
                                    MATTHEW 6:25–27

Another time Jesus said that God knows how many hairs are on your head (Matthew 10:30). Talk about intimate knowledge! Why else would God be concerned about such small matters unless He was totally involved in everything about you?

No matter how busy and distracted you get, rest assured that God always has time for you, and He's always paying attention. No matter how much you feel that nobody understands you, realize that God understands you completely. No matter how alone you feel sometimes, never forget that God loves you and cares for you. He's interested in everything about you, right down to the smallest matter in your life.

# *H o p e*

*Without wavering,*
*let us hold tightly to the hope we say we have,*
*for God can be trusted to keep his promise.*

HEBREWS 10:23

*Have* you ever thought about some of the amazing things that have been developed just in the last twenty-five years? Here's a short list of some products that didn't even exist (at least not for popular use) a quarter century ago:

Personal computers       Compact discs
The Internet             Home-delivered pizza
Fax machines             Starbucks coffee
Cellular telephones      DVD
Frequent Flyer Miles     Car navigation systems

And here are just three momentous events that have occurred during the same time span (no doubt you can think of more):

❶ The breakup of the Soviet Union and the fall of the Iron Curtain

❷ The development of a common currency in Europe

❸ The discovery of the DNA code for the human genome

You are living in the time of greatest change the world has ever known. Technology continues to race along at a breakneck pace. Social changes seem more dramatic now. And the shifting world political scene is simply amazing (if a little unsettling).

Because change is happening so rapidly, people are understandably nervous. We don't mean hand-wringing nervous (although there is plenty of that going around), but more like generally anxious as a result of all the uncertainty. Whenever you live around a lot of change—whether it's on the job, in school, in your family, or in the world—you feel insecure about the future, and it all gets very personal. You wonder what's going to happen to you and the ones you

**Bruce Bickel** spent three weeks as an aspiring actor before spending twenty years as a perspiring attorney. His flair for theatrics goes to waste in his law practice (he specializes in estate planning and probate), but Bruce is a gifted communicator. His speeches, seminars, and sermons serve as the outlet for his pent-up comedic and dramatic talents. Bruce resides in Fresno, California, with his wife, Cheryl. When he isn't doing lawyer stuff, Bruce is active at Westmont College, where he has taught and serves on the Board of Trustees.

**Stan Jantz** has been involved with Christian retail for more than twenty-five years and currently works in public relations for Berean Christian Stores. Stan and his wife, Karin, live in Fresno, where Stan is active in his church and with Youth for Christ. Stan serves on the Board of Trustees of Biola University.

**Bruce & Stan** have cowritten twenty-five books, including the international best-seller *God Is in the Small Stuff.* Their passion is to present truth in a clear, concise, and casual manner that encourages people to connect in a meaningful way with the living God.

Bruce & Stan welcome your comments and questions. Contact them at: P.O. Box 25565, Fresno, CA 93729 or guide@bruceandstan.com

Be sure to check out the Bruce & Stan Website at: www.bruceandstan.com

going to change. You just don't know what's going to happen, and neither do we. However, we can give you a big guarantee about the distant future, which begins when your earthly life ends and your eternal life kicks into gear. This is when you realize "the hope that is within you," which is God's promise that you will spend eternity with Him—as long as you have made peace with God through Jesus Christ.

As good as life on earth gets (and it can get pretty good), it's only temporary. As bad as life on earth gets (and it can get pretty bad), it's only temporary. Someday when this old world is through, God will make all things new, and we will fully become what God wants us to be. We really believe that.

Meanwhile, you have your life ahead of you. God has some wonderful things for you to do, including giving hope to others. When you meet people with no hope, remember that only Jesus can give them the hope they need. And never forget that you may be the person God uses to give it to them.

love. You may be asking:

"Will I be able to keep my job, or will I lose it in the latest round of downsizing?"

"Will I get married, and if I do, how do I know the person I marry will be right for me?"

"Will I continue to have a happy marriage, and will we ever be able to afford a house?"

"Will we ever feel completely safe in our community . . .in our country. . .in the world?"

We've been thinking about this stuff, especially as the 21$^{ST}$ century unfolds with all kinds of new uncertainties. As we look around, we've come to the conclusion that the things all of us are looking for—prosperity, happiness, and security—can really be summed up in one word: *hope.*

People are hoping against hope that everything will go well with their lives. Some people take more drastic measures to prepare for the future than others do, but everyone hopes the future will be better. This includes the foreseeable future, which are the months and years ahead, as well as the distant future, which is the time beyond your life and ours.

We can't give you any guarantees about the foreseeable future, except that it's going to be exciting because it's